HEALTHY HABITS

LOOKING AFTER MENTAL HEALTH

by Emma Carlson Berne

Consultant: Beth Gambro
Reading Specialist, Yorkville, Illinois

BEARPORT
PUBLISHING

Minneapolis, Minnesota

Teaching Tips

Before Reading
- Look at the cover of the book. Discuss the picture and the title.
- Ask readers to brainstorm a list of what they already know about mental health. What can they expect to see in the book?
- Go on a picture walk, looking through the pictures to discuss vocabulary and make predictions about the text.

During Reading
- Read for purpose. Encourage readers to think about their own mental health habits as they are reading.
- Ask readers to look for the details of the book. What are they learning about how to take care of their mental health?
- If readers encounter an unknown word, ask them to look at the sounds in the word. Then, ask them to look at the rest of the page. Are there any clues to help them understand?

After Reading
- Encourage readers to pick a buddy and reread the book together.
- Ask readers to name two reasons to make looking after their mental health a habit. Find the pages that tell about these things.
- Ask readers to write or draw something they learned about taking care of their mental health.

Credits:
Cover and title page, © pkline/iStock, © mitsuap/Shutterstock; 3, © vetre/Adobe Stock; 5, © lovelyday12/Adobe Stock; 7, © SDI Productions/iStock; 8-9, © alkir/iStock; 11, © WavebreakmediaMicro/Adobe Stock; 12-13, © PeopleImages/iStock; 15, © PeopleImages/iStock; 16-17, © Ilike/Adobe Stock; 19, © Mtaitas/Shutterstock; 20-21, © FatCamera/iStock; 22T, © Samuel B./Adobe Stock; 22M, © EVAfotografie/iStock; 22B, © SDI Productions/iStock; 23TL, © Pixel-Shot/Shutterstock; 23TM, © alexei_tm/Adobe Stock; 23TR, © pixdeluxe/iStock; 23BL, © Weekend Images Inc./iStock; 23BR, © Sunny studio/Adobe Stock.

STATEMENT ON USAGE OF GENERATIVE ARTIFICIAL INTELLIGENCE
Bearport Publishing remains committed to publishing high-quality nonfiction books. Therefore, we restrict the use of generative AI to ensure accuracy of all text and visual components pertaining to a book's subject. See BearportPublishing.com for details.

Library of Congress Cataloging-in-Publication Data

Names: Berne, Emma Carlson, 1979- author.
Title: Looking after mental health / Emma Carlson Berne ; consultant, Beth
  Gambro, Reading Specialist, Yorkville, Illinois.
Description: Minneapolis, Minnesota : Bearport Publishing Company, [2024] |
  Series: Healthy habits | Includes bibliographical references and index.
Identifiers: LCCN 2023028234 (print) | LCCN 2023028235 (ebook) | ISBN
  9798889162445 (library binding) | ISBN 9798889162513 (paperback) | ISBN
  9798889162575 (ebook)
Subjects: LCSH: Mental health--Juvenile literature.
Classification: LCC RA790 .B455 2024 (print) | LCC RA790 (ebook) | DDC
  362.2--dc23/eng/20230710
LC record available at https://lccn.loc.gov/2023028234
LC ebook record available at https://lccn.loc.gov/2023028235

Copyright © 2024 Bearport Publishing Company. All rights reserved. No part of this publication may be reproduced in whole or in part, stored in any retrieval system, or transmitted in any form or by any means, electronic, mechanical, photocopying, recording, or otherwise, without written permission from the publisher.
For more information, write to Bearport Publishing, 5357 Penn Avenue South, Minneapolis, MN 55419.

Contents

Taking Care of Me 4

Make It a Habit 22
Glossary 23
Index 24
Read More 24
Learn More Online......................... 24
About the Author 24

Taking Care of Me

Sometimes, the world gets very busy.

I stop and take a breath.

This is good for my mental health.

5

There are many ways I take care of myself.

I look after my mental health every day.

That makes it a **habit**!

Mental health is about feeling good in my mind.

It has to do with how I am thinking.

Mental health helps me take care of my feelings.

Mental health has a lot to do with **emotions**.

Inside, I have so many feelings!

All of them are okay.

But some feelings can make it hard to do things.

Sometimes, I have big emotions.

So, I talk to someone I trust.

This helps me think about what to do.

Feeling **relaxed** is good for my mental health.

I read a book or listen to music to calm down.

Playing with my friends is fun!

Spending time with people I love makes me happy.

It is good for me, too.

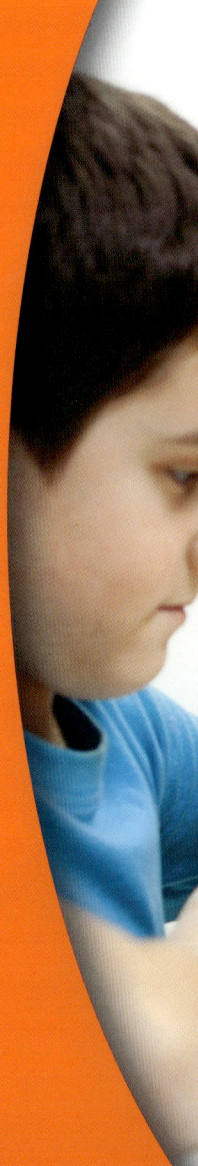

A healthy body helps me have a healthy mind.

Exercise gives me **energy**.

So does getting enough sleep.

These things help me all day long!

Taking care of my mind feels good.

I look after my mental health every day.

It is a healthy habit!

Make It a Habit

A habit is something you do every day. What are ways we can make taking care of our mental health a habit?

Spend some time outside every day. It can help you relax.

Find things that make you happy, and do them!

Check in on your feelings every day. Are you having big emotions?

Glossary

emotions strong feelings

energy the power to do things, such as work or run

exercise activity done to stay fit and healthy

habit something done regularly

relaxed feeling rested and calm

Index

emotions 10, 12
energy 18
feelings 8, 10, 14, 20, 22
habit 6, 20, 22
mind 8, 18, 20
relax 14, 22

Read More

Chang, Kirsten. *Understanding Emotions (A Healthy Life).* Minneapolis: Bellwether Media, 2022.

Harper, Reggie. *Sometimes We Feel Sad (Dealing with Your Feelings).* New York: Cavendish Square Publishing, 2022.

Learn More Online

1. Go to **www.factsurfer.com** or scan the QR code below.
2. Enter **"Healthy Habits Mental Health"** into the search box.
3. Click on the cover of this book to see a list of websites.

About the Author

Emma Carlson Berne lives with her family in Cincinnati, Ohio. When she feels stressed, she takes a walk around the block.